The Gayer-Anderson Cat

Neal Spencer

D1410525

THE BRITISH MUSEUM PRESS

For Martha

First published in 2007 by
The British Museum Press
A division of The British Museum
Company Ltd
38 Russell Square
London WC1B 3QQ

Reprinted 2010
www.britishmuseum.org

A catalogue record for this book is available from the British Library

ISBN: 978-0-7141-1973-1

Designed by Esterson Associates
Typeset in Miller and
Akzidenz-Grotesque
Printed and bound in China
by C&C Offset Printing Co., Ltd

Map by Claire Thorne

Acknowledgements
Thanks are due to Vivian Davies for his support for this book and the accompanying scientific research; to Richard Parkinson and John Taylor for useful discussions about the Gayer-Anderson Cat; and especially to Patricia Usick for her help with the archives relating to the bequest. Also in the Department of Ancient Egypt and Sudan, thanks are due to Claire Thorne and Evan York. In the Department of Conservation, Documentation and Science, David Saunders supported the scientific investigations, undertaken by Janet Ambers, Sue La Niece, Duncan Hook, Andrew Middleton, Antony Simpson and Fleur Shearman, who also provided invaluable information on ancient metallurgy. Lisa Baylis shot the wonderful new photographs. Nicholas Warner and Theo Gayer-Anderson were very helpful with providing information on Major Gayer-Anderson and his house in Cairo, and access to his unpublished memoirs. Lyn Longridge provided useful pointers on her late grandmother, Mary Stout. The editors Laura Lappin and Felicity Maunder saw the book through to press. Finally, I would like to thank the volunteers who helped collect pharaonic feline material for the book: Margie Pelayo, Samuel-Louis Gardiner, Joe Cable, Azharul Chowdhury and Robert Freestone.

Contents

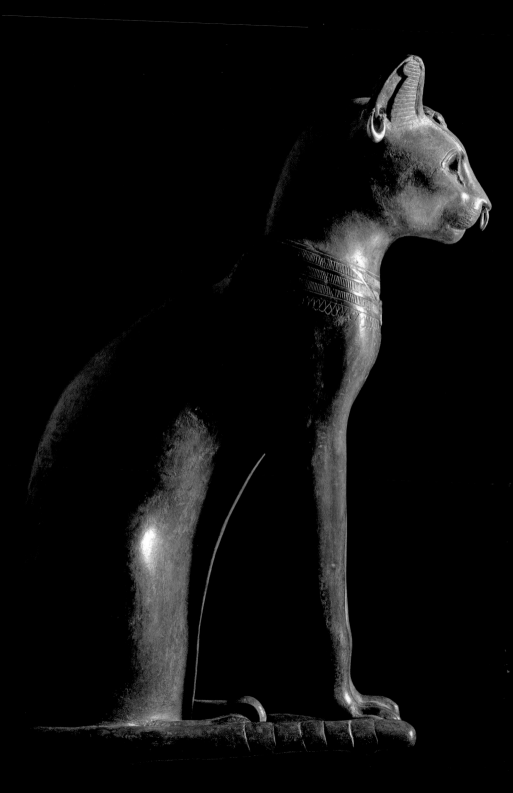

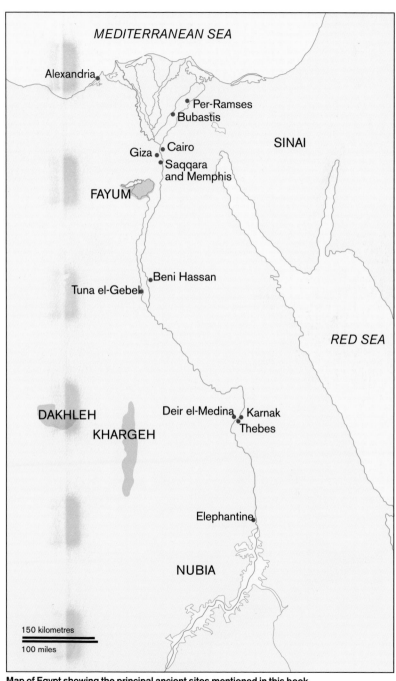

MEDITERRANEAN SEA

Alexandria

Per-Ramses
Bubastis

SINAI

Giza Cairo
Saqqara
and Memphis

FAYUM

Beni Hassan
Tuna el-Gebel

RED SEA

DAKHLEH

KHARGEH

Deir el-Medina Karnak
Thebes

Elephantine

NUBIA

150 kilometres

100 miles

Map of Egypt showing the principal ancient sites mentioned in this book.

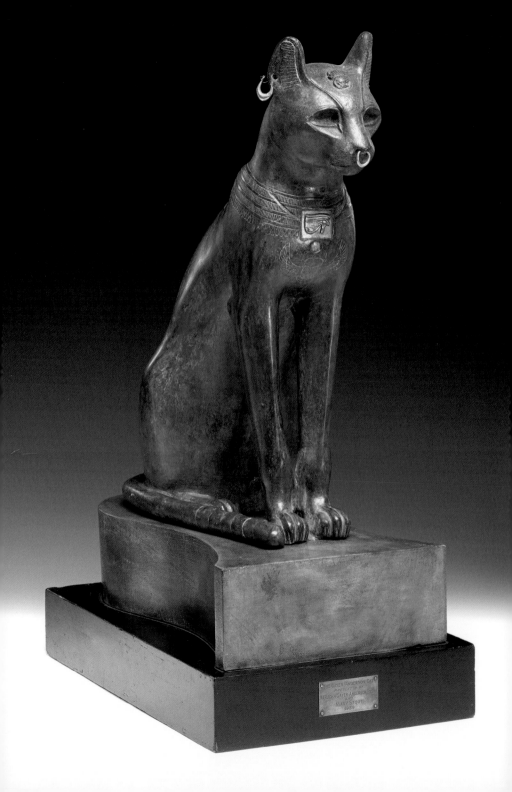

Chapter One
Introduction

1 The Gayer-Anderson Cat on display base with plaque.

The bronze, roughly life-size figurine known as the Gayer-Anderson Cat has enchanted visitors to the British Museum ever since it was first put on display shortly after the Second World War. The ancient artist's faithful rendering of the feline form, and the skill involved in casting such an aesthetically pleasing figure, undoubtedly account for some of the object's prestige. But the Cat also hints at the exoticism of ancient Egypt, and especially its religion. To modern people a cat is rarely anything other than a pet, but to Egyptians of the pharaonic era it could also be the manifestation of a god. This book presents the Gayer-Anderson Cat both as one of the finest examples of metal casting known from the ancient world, and as a religious object with a specific purpose.

Well-known and loved objects at the British Museum often reveal new secrets, even after decades or centuries on display. The opportunity to undertake modern scientific examinations of the Cat, in the Museum's laboratories, came when the Egyptian galleries were being redeveloped. For several days the Cat underwent a range of non-invasive analyses which have yielded new information about the method of its manufacture, and also about some of the restoration work undertaken before its arrival at the British Museum.

The Cat is unusual among the millions of objects in the British Museum for another reason. Very few pieces bear the name of an individual in the manner of 'the Gayer-Anderson Cat'. The final chapter gives a brief account of the life of the British Army major Robert Grenville Gayer-Anderson, and the interesting, if somewhat stressful, 'life' of the Cat after he first set eyes upon it in Cairo, one autumn morning in 1934.

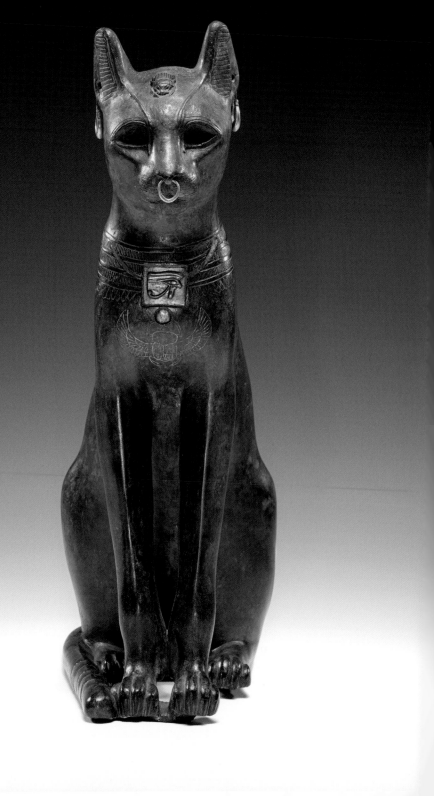

Chapter Two
The Gayer-Anderson Cat

The Gayer-Anderson Cat sits on its rear legs, serenely gazing forwards, with its tail drawn up by its right side. This 42 cm-tall metal figurine embodies many of the aesthetic qualities of ancient Egyptian art, with master craftsmanship that combines both attention to natural detail and the symbolism required of a religious, sacred object.

The Cat's head is exquisitely modelled. Unusually among the thousands of surviving bronze cats, in this example the head is held slightly downwards, rather than gazing upwards as is more common. The eye cavities dominate the face; originally these would have been inlaid with glass, faience, precious stone (perhaps rock crystal) or metals. At the inner corners of the eyes the canthi are indicated. A thinly incised eyebrow and a raised outer line give the eyes an almost hieroglyphic appearance. From between the eyes, two raised lines run towards the ears, probably an abstracted rendition of the striping of a cat's fur in this area. On close inspection, the naturalism of the ears is in fact laden with religious symbolism, as each ear contains a raised relief feather, stylizing (and reinterpreting) the fine hairs found inside the ear of a cat. The particular shape of the feather would have been recognizable to the ancient Egyptians as the symbol of the goddess Maat, who embodied truth and righteousness.

Further religious symbolism is found on the head, where a scarab beetle sits between the two ears. Though cast as part of the whole statue, the beetle is depicted in detail, with striations on the rear part of its body, and six legs. It has been suggested that placing a scarab here also echoed fur patterns on living cats, but its religious symbolism was clearly paramount. The scarab was seen to embody the morning sun, and to be a manifestation of the god Khepri. As the rising sun intimated notions of rebirth, the scarab was also a powerful symbol of funerary beliefs. Other bronze cat

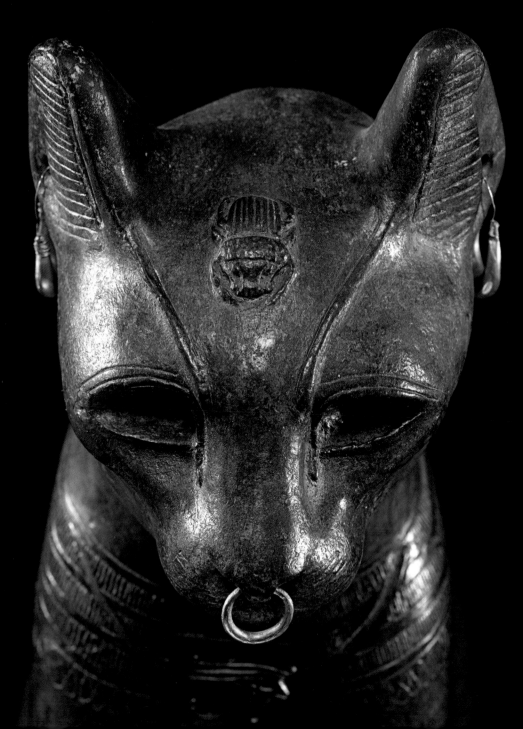

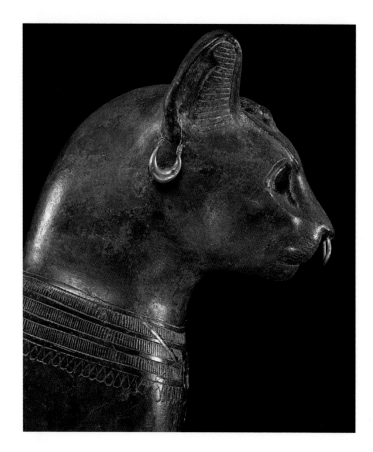

figures have a scarab motif incised on the forehead, or even
inlaid in different materials such as faience or ivory.

The Cat's elegant nose sits above a pursed mouth, framed
by incised whiskers. Both the ears and the nose are pierced,
and now sport small gold rings. The wire holding the
earrings in place is modern, but the rings themselves are
undoubtedly ancient. Their distinctive lunate form is found
on several other cats whose earrings survive. Many ancient
cat figurines have nose and ear piercings, but the earrings
rarely survive, as they are liable to break off during the
burial or excavation of the figurines, and are attractive
items for thieves. A photograph taken by Gayer-Anderson
in Cairo during the 1930s shows the Cat wearing much
larger simple rings in both ears (see fig. 32). These are not

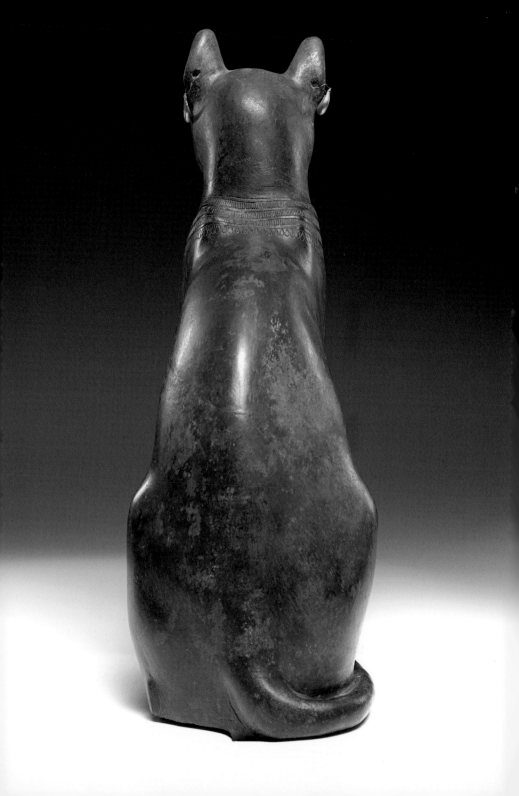

5 *Left* The Gayer-Anderson Cat: rear view.

6 *Right* The Gayer-Anderson Cat: detail of the head and chest.

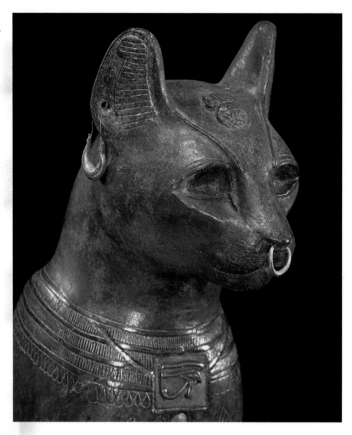

British Museum's collections, so the present rings must have been placed on the figure by Gayer-Anderson before his death in 1945, or perhaps by his brother, Thomas, or his friend Mary Stout before it was given to the British Museum in 1947. Nonetheless, the form of the rings now on the Cat does match those found on other bronze cats. Rings of this shape have been found in late first millennium BC contexts at Memphis, and at Tanis, Defenneh and Athribis in the Delta.

Although the rest of the Cat's body does not contain the detailing evident on the head, it is nonetheless finely modelled. Viewing the Cat from the rear makes the craftsman's skill evident, particularly in the execution of the shoulder blades, spine and ribcage. The relaxed, yet alert,

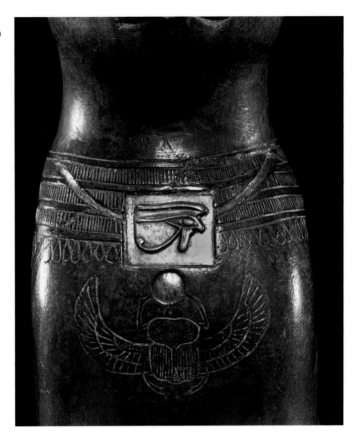

pose of the Cat is well conveyed by the subtly undulating surface planes of the main body; less well accomplished examples show a more geometric, hard-edged rendering of the chest area. The asymmetry of the sculpture is most apparent in the rear view (fig. 5), another example of the observational detail evident in so much Egyptian art: no living cat is perfectly symmetrical.

A four-part collar sits below the Cat's neck, representing three bands of closely spaced rectangular beads, above a necklace of drop-shaped pendants. Such complex collars, made of faience and precious stone beads, and sometimes floral elements, are commonly depicted being worn by men and women in tomb scenes, but are also an important part of the adornment of mummies and anthropomorphic coffins.

A necklace is inlaid over this four-part collar, from which appears to hang a small rectangular plaque (fig. 7). The necklace string is inlaid with silver, and the plaque itself is carved from silver, with a raised relief depiction of the *udjat*-eye. The *udjat*-eye, a stylized representation of a human eye, with eyebrow above and the markings of a falcon's feathers beneath, was a powerful religious symbol in ancient Egypt. It was closely associated with several ancient myths, notably that of the eye of Horus, a god often shown in the form of a falcon. The gods Horus and Seth were engaged in a series of struggles over the succession to their father's throne. In one episode, the evil Seth rips Horus's left eye out, which is later restored by their sister (or mother) Isis. The eye thus embodies the notion of restorative, healing power, and could also be seen as a protective symbol. Thousands of amulets in this form survive, and would evidently be worn by individuals to ward off evil powers and illness. That real pets could be adorned with necklaces and earrings is clear from a scene in the tomb of Penbuy and Kasa at Deir el-Medina in Thebes. Some cats wear necklaces in the form of a string of cowrie-shells. Many bronze cat figurines are adorned with an *aegis* hanging from a necklace, an insignia found at the front and rear of divine boats, but also associated with various goddesses. Other cats wear a figure of a goddess around their neck.

Beneath the *udjat*-eye amulet is another depiction of a scarab, this time simply incised into the surface of the metal. The beetle, with individual body elements faithfully depicted, is adorned with two falcon wings and a small sun-disc inlaid with silver. Once again, solar symbolism is paramount, with the wings alluding to the creator god Horus, or perhaps a solar form, Ra-Horakhty, and the scarab being a manifestation of Khepri, as with the example found on the head of the Cat.

The Cat's legs taper inwards to allow the front paws to sit side by side, a clever device employed by the artist to improve the stability of the object. Both front and back legs bear details of the individual claws, here shown as if partly unsheathed from the surrounding skin (see fig. 27).

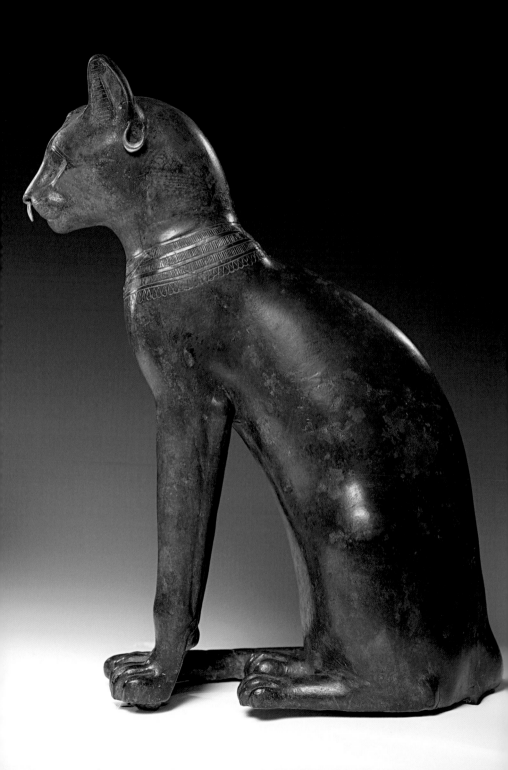

The structure of the taut legs is further suggested by the modelling of the carpal (or wrist) bones and the long ulna bone. The hip bones of the rear legs are hinted at through the shape of the Cat's body.

The tail of the Cat lies by its right side, again ensuring that the object is not too fragile, and ends to the side of its right paw. Egyptian cat statues always have the tail brought up on this side, which reflects the convention by which animals were depicted in reliefs, paintings and especially hieroglyphs: the dominant orientation featured the animal facing right. If the tail lay on the other side of the statue, it would not be visible in this typical view, and thus the depiction would not be a faithful rendering of the cat's most distinguishing features. The final part of the tail is divided into six segments (see fig. 27), a detail intended to convey the striping found on some cats' tails. The rest of the body appears smooth, though modern surface cleaning and polishing may have removed traces of further incision or even stippling to indicate fur.

Only one of the two tangs beneath the Cat survives. Formed during the casting process (see fig. 25), these allowed the figure to be secured to its ancient base, which does not survive but would have been made of wood or metal. The cat currently sits on a wooden base, commissioned by Gayer-Anderson in the 1930s (see fig. 1). Its form replicates that found on other ancient Egyptian bronze cat figurines, where it is sometimes cast as one with the animal (usually on smaller figures), or can be made of wood. The distinctive shape echoes that of the *menat-*counterpoise, which balanced the weight of heavy necklaces worn by goddesses and the elite. This symbol was closely linked to the goddess Hathor.

Cats in ancient Egypt: pets and manifestations of gods
Wild cats have been found in prehistoric cemeteries in Egypt, but there is evidence that by 1850 BC domesticated cats were being kept as pets. Shown in tomb reliefs, the cat usually sits beneath the chair of the tomb-owner's wife. Dogs are more commonly depicted, and monkeys and geese also appear. Unlike dogs however, cats are rarely named in

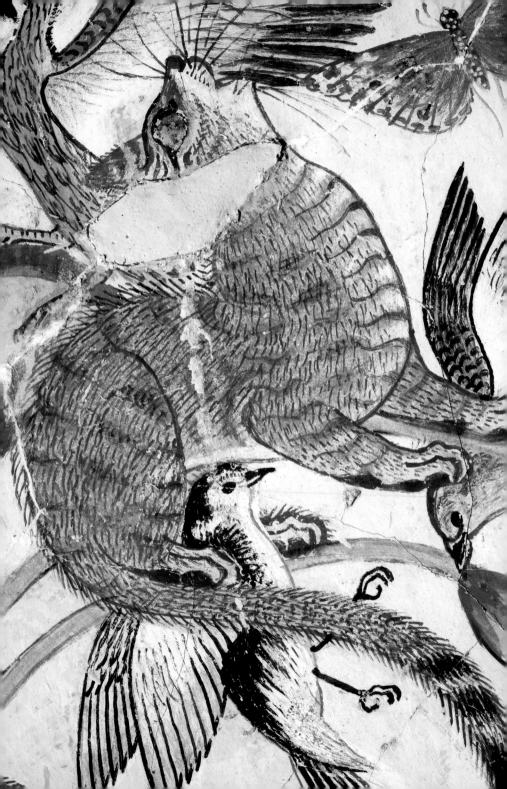

these scenes. Cats, whether the African wild cat (*Felix silvestris libyca*), its domesticated form, or some of the other less common species (*felix chaus* and *felix serval*) were all called *miu* in ancient Egyptian, a word that echoes the sound cats make. The popularity of cats is reflected in the use of this word to make up personal names for both men and women, for example *Pa-miu* ('the tomcat'), a name found from the fifteenth century BC onwards. The cat of Prince Tuthmosis, son of Amenhotep III, was simply named *Ta-miit* ('the female cat'). Its limestone sarcophagus is inscribed with texts identifying the dead cat as 'the Osiris', the main god of the afterlife, as with elite human burials. At Abydos, seventeen cats were found buried in a chamber within a small mud-brick pyramid, accompanied by crude offering bowls. Finely painted tombs of the Middle and New Kingdoms often feature depictions of cats, whether lurking in the papyrus marshes, stalking birds or even raiding their nests for eggs. A fabulous example from the

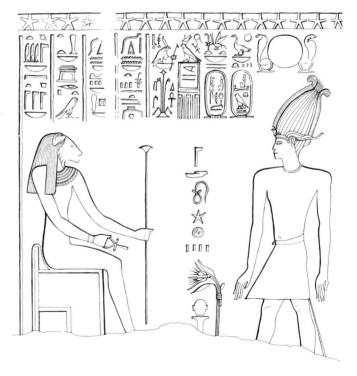

19

tomb of Nebamun shows a cat resting on papyrus stalks capturing a bird's wing in its jaws (fig. 9). While such scenes may reflect the affection shown towards cats, they should not be read as simply 'snapshots' of domestic life, as there was much underlying religious symbolism to these scenes.

Satirical papyri and sketches on ostraca sometimes cast cats in the role of humans: drinking, shepherding livestock (fig. 12) or playing games. A reversal of the traditional roles of cat and mouse is also found in such sketches: an army of mice attacks a fort defended by cats, or cats wait upon a noble mouse lady! While revealing something of ancient humour, these images are not bereft of religious symbolism, as they evoke a chaotic world to be avoided at all costs.

The Gayer-Anderson Cat is no house pet or player in a satirical scene. Rather, it is a manifestation of a specific god. Egyptian religion has left us many striking depictions of their gods, in tomb scenes, upon temple walls, and on many other types of object. Gods can be depicted as animals, or as hybrid forms mixing parts of one animal with those of another. To many, the animal-headed gods typify the exotic nature of Egyptian religion. However, the Egyptians did not actually believe that their gods were falcons, cats, snakes or any other earthly form. Rather they thought that, in certain circumstances, gods would manifest themselves in the guise of familiar creatures, man-made objects such as statues, or even inanimate natural features such as mountains. The form chosen would often reflect an aspect of that god's personality, for example the strength of the bull in the case of the god Montu. Qualities could be both positive and negative; the potentially fatal power of the hippopotamus needed to be controlled, but the vision of, and flying height attained by, the falcon was something to admire. And so it was not thought illogical that one god could manifest in several forms: the creator god Amun-Ra could take the form of a man, a goose or a ram.

By the Middle Kingdom, the cat had become associated with the sun-god. The texts adorning finely painted wooden coffins sometimes described the sun-god as a cat. Later, *Book of the Dead* papyri depict cats brandishing knives, ready to avert any danger to the deceased's progression

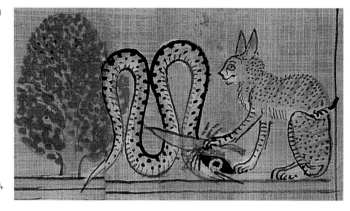

11 *Right* Detail showing the cat slaying the Apophis serpent, from the *Book of the Dead* of Hunefer. Thebes, c. 1300 BC.

12 *Below* Detail of a cat leading a flock of geese, from a satirical papyrus. Deir el-Medina, c. 1250 BC.

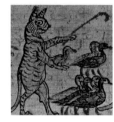

through the afterlife. One well-known vignette features a cat killing the evil Apophis serpent in front of the sacred *ished*-tree, a battle the sun-god had to fight continuously to ensure the dawn of a new day (fig. 11). Elsewhere in the same texts, cat-headed guardians protected the gateways between the different hours of the night, through which the sun-god and the deceased were expected to proceed before morning rebirth. Some stelae dedicated by craftsmen living in the workmen's village at Deir el-Medina show the sun-god in the form of a seated cat. Cats could also perform a protective role: they appear on the magical ivory wands placed in tombs of the Middle Kingdom, and on steatite wands of a later date. Both types of object served a protective purpose, particularly with regard to children and the deceased. The placing of faience figurines of crouching cats in tombs of the First Intermediate Period further suggests protection of the dead.

The Gayer-Anderson Cat probably represents not the sun-god, but one of the other gods who were depicted as felines. The lioness, with her evident strength and prowess at hunting, was associated with various gods from early on in Egyptian civilization, notably Hathor, Neith, Tefnut, Pakhet, Mut and Bastet. In temple reliefs, Bastet is always shown as a woman with the head of a lioness (fig. 10), reflecting the ferocious, terrifying aspect of these deities, and especially her association with Sekhmet ('the powerful one'; fig. 13). One myth, *The Destruction of Mankind*, relates

13 Granodiorite statue of the goddess Sekhmet, *c.* **1360 BC.**

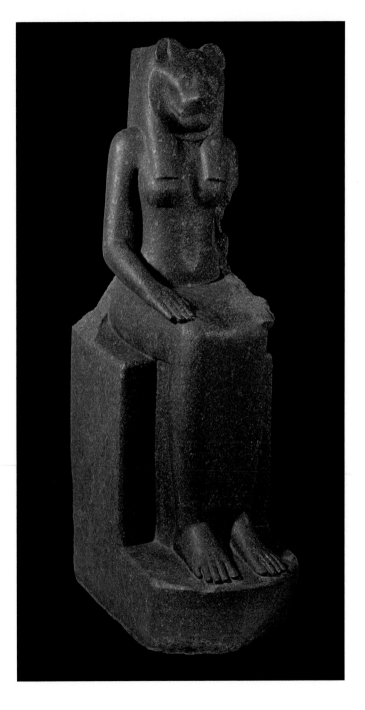

how Sekhmet sought to destroy humanity as punishment for man's misdeeds, but was tricked by the sun-god into drinking beer dyed red, thinking it was human blood. The goddess fell asleep through drunkenness, and mankind was spared. In another, the *Myth of the Eye of Ra*, the 'eye of Ra' manifests itself as a raging lioness who leaves Egypt, later to be pacified by Thoth and return appeased as a cat: 'She is furious as Sekhmet, and she is contented as Bastet.'

In contrast to lions, the serenity of cats, their fertility in producing offspring and subsequent maternal care when nursing their young must have been qualities associated with other aspects of some of those gods. The ability of cats to hunt rodents and snakes also would have been recognized, alongside their night vision. From around 950 BC, it was the goddess Bastet who took the form of a cat in bronze figurines and other small objects, offering a stark contrast to her vicious Sekhmet-like form found in temple reliefs. Bastet is often characterized as the 'eye of Ra', whether in her leonine or feline form. The scarab upon the Gayer-Anderson Cat's head has clear solar allusions, with its connotations of daily rebirth, so it is likely that this statue represents Bastet. The return of the eye of Ra in a peaceful form was the subject of annual festivals throughout Egypt. Protective amulets, sacred cat coffins and other objects which reflected religious beliefs through a wider tranche of the population always depict Bastet in the form of a cat, or a cat-headed woman.

Of course, other goddesses could be depicted as cats (a sandstone statue of a cat inscribed for Mut was set up outside her temple at Karnak), but this was much less common. The Gayer-Anderson Cat may not even represent a single god: Egyptian religion is very complex, and gods were often merged, or syncretized, in a process that would create a new divinity which embodied aspects of the original gods. One bronze cat found at Saqqara is named, in the text incised upon its base, as Hathor-Bastet. Hathor was closely associated with the process of childbirth, and acted as a goddess of joy, music, fertility and the household. The presence of small cats adorning sistra (sacred rattles) also attests to the close association of Bastet and Hathor.

Bastet-Isis was another common fusion of divinities, still worshipped in Roman times, and a statue of Mut-Sekhmet-Bastet has survived. It is possible that the Gayer-Anderson Cat represents one of these deities, combining Bastet with another god.

When was the Gayer-Anderson Cat made?
The loss of the original base, and thus any text which might have been carved or painted upon it, removes one of the key pieces of dating evidence for the Gayer-Anderson Cat. Inscriptions on bronze statuettes are rather standard and brief, often just giving the name of the dedicant, his parents and the god, without titles. If the Cat bore the name of a king, or a well-known official, it might be possible to say with some precision exactly when the object was made. The style of the hieroglyphs, and the changing fashion for names, would allow us to place it within a certain period. Other dating methods are available to the Egyptologist. First, a consideration of the type of object: bronze figurines of deities are rarely found before the first millennium BC. Secondly, the location where the object was found can help, as other pieces, especially pottery, from the same context may be datable. Alas, the provenance of the Cat is unknown. Thousands of bronze cat figurines survive from ancient Egypt, but very few are inscribed or come from scientific excavations, so the archaeological context is lost. The majority of bronzes were acquired on the art market, having been removed from temples and cemeteries, especially during the uncontrolled plundering of these sites in the nineteenth century. Thirdly, scientific analysis can help, for example radio-carbon dating of wooden objects. While thermoluminescence can be used on the core found inside hollow-cast statues, the amount of modern treatment undergone by the Cat means that the results would provide a very broad date range of little use. Finally, stylistic parallels with other similar, closely dated, objects can help. But in this case, that is not easy. The unique nature of such cast metal statues makes dating on stylistic grounds difficult: once cast, the original wax prototype and the surrounding investiture into which the molten metal was

poured were destroyed (see chapter four). Thus no two cats are identical, and significant variation is possible even within a short time at the same place of production. The statues are often assigned to the very broad periods in which these sites were occupied, for example 'Late Period', a part of Egyptian history that spans over three centuries. It is like looking at a painting and not being sure if it was made in 1707 or 2007!

While not helping to offer a narrow date, some parallels deserve consideration. A cat in the Musée du Louvre, Paris, bears an inscription with the name of the king Psamtek I (664–610 BC), and the official who donated it. Though the composition of the figure broadly matches that of the Gayer-Anderson Cat, its head is held high, it wears an *aegis* topped with a feline head, hung off a pearl necklace, and the tail is arranged differently, bending around the front of the right paw. The eyes are inlaid with stone and outlined in faience. But should we be looking at stylistic differences over time, or might regional variations play a greater role?

What about non-royal inscriptions? Very few of the thousands of surviving bronze cats bear an inscription on the base. This is often because the original wooden or metal base has not survived. The form of the earrings on the Gayer-Anderson Cat cannot be used as a dating criterion, as they are not original to the object. In light of its size and another inscribed example now in Cairo, found in the Serapeum at Saqqara, a 26th Dynasty (664–525 BC) date seems most likely. However, one cannot rule out a date in the following two centuries.

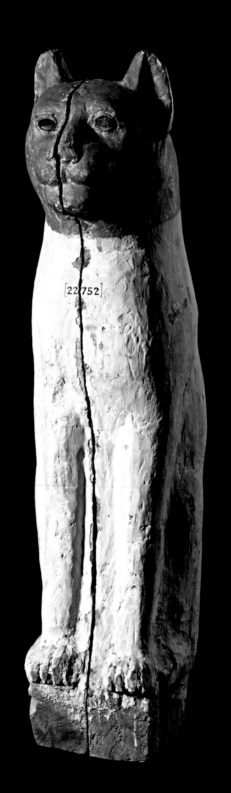

Chapter Three
Sacred animals: donors, temples and mass burials

14 Wooden coffin of a cat, perhaps from Bubastis, c. 1st century BC–1st century AD.

A statue dedicated in a temple?

It is extremely unlikely that the Gayer-Anderson Cat was the main cult image in a temple of Bastet. Although a cult image in the form of a seated cat is depicted upon a shrine of the 30th Dynasty from Saft el-Henna, we know from inscriptions that such statues were usually much larger than the 42-cm-tall Gayer-Anderson Cat, and often inlaid with a variety of precious stones and gilded. Due to the value of these materials, cult statues almost never survive. Our Cat is more likely to have been a votive statue, dedicated by a king or wealthy individual to mark his piety and to provide access to the god.

In the first millennium BC, the production of votive bronze figures reached incredible levels, with thousands of these statues being purchased and dedicated by pious individuals at various temple sites. Cat statues in other materials are very rare (a few stone ones and a plaster example are known), in contrast to the abundant number of stone statues of lions or falcons set up in temples.

Where extant, inscriptions on the bases of these bronze statues usually give the donor's name and profession, and sometimes the name of his or her parents. Inscriptions found on some figures suggest that they were dedicated on specific festival days, such as the New Year (small figures of Bastet can be inscribed with a New Year greeting) or the anniversary of the king's coronation. More frequently, they simply invoke the god's name and occasionally contain a simple wish or request. So a devotee of Bastet might purchase a cat figurine to dedicate in a temple, in the hope of asking the goddess to cure illness, ensure successful childbirth, or even to seek the solution to a specific problem. The practice of dedicating statues continued through the Ptolemaic and Roman eras: votives for Bastet dedicated by people with Greek names have survived.

27

The fine quality of the Gayer-Anderson Cat does indicate that it was commissioned rather than being one of the thousands of bronze cats offered for sale in and around temples: some of these are poorly modelled and made of badly cast metal. Access to materials and craftsmanship of this quality would suggest that the donor was from the upper levels of a priesthood, the military, the civil administration, or perhaps closely attached to the royal court (officials often held simultaneous positions in all four areas). Surviving texts tell us of the lavish donations given to temples by pharaohs as a mark of piety towards the gods. One inscription, of King Osorkon I, refers to a vast range of cult statues and ritual objects made of gold, silver, electrum and inlaid bronze, amounting to at least 209 tonnes of precious metals. Royal donations were complemented by those of wealthy officials, priests and military persons. The securely dated bronze cat now in the Louvre, 28 cm tall and inscribed with the cartouches of Psamtek I (664–610 BC), also bears a dedicatory text. This tells us that Mer-sopdu, son of Hor, offered the statue to receive protection from Bastet. It also specifies that the temple dancer Djed-bastet-iwefankh was responsible for the statue once it was placed in the temple.

Various cat forms appear among the thousands of bronze statues which survive. In addition to the seated cat, there are a few examples of standing or striding cats, but a very common type shows Bastet as a cat-headed woman (fig. 15). In these figurines, she holds a sistrum, an *aegis* or a basket, and wears an elaborately patterned ankle-length dress. Smaller compositions in metal featuring a prostrate cat with her kittens feeding are also common, highlighting the fertility and maternal nature of the animal. Amulets of cats are found in vast numbers, in materials such as amethyst, calcite, red cornelian and chalcedony; the smaller bronze figurines of seated cats were often fitted with a loop on their back for suspension. This allowed the figures to be worn on a necklace or attached to temple walls or sacred equipment. These amulets again reflected the popular view of the cat as a protective and fertile animal. Some people went further, taking a name that referred to Bastet: Pa-di-bastet was a

15 Bronze figure
of Bastet as a cat-
headed woman,
inscribed for the
donor Pef-tjawy-bast,
c. 2nd–1st century BC.

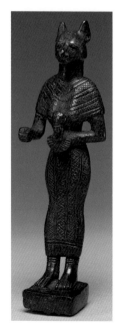

name fashionable from around 600 BC, and literally means 'He whom Bastet gave'.

The temples in and around which the votive statues were dedicated must have become quite cluttered. In the Khargeh Oasis, a rare example of bronze statues found in their original location was discovered: a room in the small 27th Dynasty temple at Ayn Manawir yielded 360 bronze statues, mostly of Osiris. Some were still attached to their wooden bases, and the room also contained wooden boxes which held other equipment. Some of the finer and larger statues, such as the Gayer-Anderson Cat, were probably housed in small wooden shrines set up in the temple grounds.

Periodically the statues were collected and buried within caches in or near the temple precincts, where it was thought that they could still benefit from rituals enacted in the temple. The statues were occasionally wrapped carefully in linen before being deposited, and sometimes even placed within wooden shrines. Caches of bronzes have been discovered at Buto, Sais, Memphis and especially Saqqara, often containing a wide variety of statues made over a long period of time (fig. 19). Alongside bronze statuary, mirrors and plaques, wooden and stone objects were often placed in the same pits. At the Serapeum at Saqqara, burial place of the Apis bulls, a huge amount of bronze statuary was buried beneath the paving stones of the avenue linking the two temples. In some cases over three hundred statues were grouped together, perhaps as part of a clearing operation before the new temple was built in the fourth century BC. The variation in quality was enormous, from 50 cm-high statues of Osiris inlaid with gold to small, crude figurines of the same god. Similar variety was evident in the gods represented: Apis, Bes, Isis, Ptah, Imhotep, Nefertem, Horus, Thoth, Hathor, Bastet and so on. The cats were inscribed for the goddess 'Bastet lady of Ankhtawy'. North of the 5th Dynasty pyramid of Userkaf, another cache was found, containing bronze, stone and wood figurines, alongside a small amount of pottery and some coins. Five of the sixty-one bronze figures depicted cats. Bronze figures of cats were even recovered from the ibis galleries at Tuna el-Gebel in Middle Egypt. Human burials also could be accompanied by bronze statuettes, though usually only figures of Osiris, principal god of the afterlife.

Which temple would the Gayer-Anderson Cat have been dedicated in? It has been associated with Saqqara, where an important cult of Bastet existed, but Bubastis is also a likely provenance. However, any of the temples dedicated to other goddesses associated with cats could have been provided with statues of the animal, so we will probably never know where the Cat was set up.

16 Bronze figure of Osiris-Iah, dedicated by Pashertaihet, 7th–4th century BC.

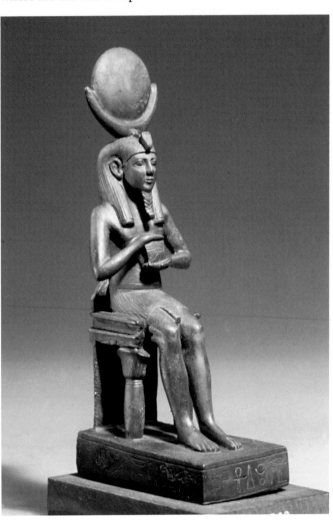

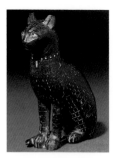

17 Bronze figurine of a cat, inlaid with gold, 7th–4th century BC.

Alternatively, the Cat may have been part of an item of sacred temple furniture. Egyptian temples not only housed statues representing gods and kings, but also standards, emblems and other equipment, all of which could be made of lavish materials and act as supports for groups of statues. Some of these objects were also inscribed with the name and titles of their donor. Sacred barques, or boats, were used to house the main divine objects when they were taken outside the sanctuary during festivals: priests would carry the barque supported by poles. Few of these survive, but we know from depictions in temples that the decks of these boats, some of which measured 68 metres in length, could be adorned with numerous emblems, standards and smaller statues of kings and gods. Could the Cat be from such a piece of temple equipment? A model barque in the Musée du Louvre, Paris, features a small bronze cat sitting on its deck. In this case, the cat would not have been provided with a base, but rather its tangs would have been inserted directly into the deck of the sacred boat. Temple reliefs also indicate that cats, perhaps in pairs or groups of four, were positioned around the base of single columns. These columns had capitals in the form of the goddess Hathor, closely associated with love and fertility, but also involved in the myths relating to Sekhmet and the *Destruction of Mankind*. A cat such as this one would not have looked out of place in such a context.

Or intended for a sacred animal cemetery?

Rather than being set up in a temple, the Gayer-Anderson Cat might have come from a sacred cat cemetery, and its interior cavity may even have been used to house a cat mummy (see fig. 26). It should be stressed that there is no clear dividing line between cemetery and temple, as animal cemeteries were provided with temples.

The ritual burial of animals, including cattle, elephants and crocodiles, took place from the earliest times in ancient Egyptian history. While gods could take on the guise of a particular creature, not all living animals were seen as sacred beings. Individual animals could be considered sacred and worshipped as such during their lifetime,

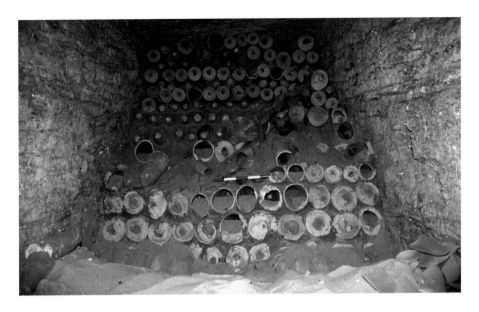

18 Ibis burials in pots in the catacombs at Saqqara, 4th–1st century BC.

occasionally being afforded a sumptuous burial fit for a king. These were the 'living *ba*' of that god. *Ba* is an Egyptian word that seems to have embodied the concept of the individual essence of a person, or in this case a god. The best example of this phenomenon is the Apis bull, identified from early on in ancient Egyptian civilization. By 1380 BC the bull lived in a finely built and decorated building within the temple of Ptah at Memphis, near modern Cairo, and was the subject of priestly rituals and cults, as with any god. Upon dying, the divine bull received full funerary rites, including a lengthy embalming process, before being buried inside a stone sarcophagus, accompanied by precious jewellery and funerary goods, in tombs at the cemetery of Saqqara.

Individual cats do not seem to have ever been seen as 'living gods'. During the first millennium BC, there is a massive rise in the number of animal burials, with literally millions of animals being interred, often in vast underground catacombs containing millions of mummies, or in reused tombs. It has been estimated that one complex of catacombs at Saqqara received 10,000 ibis mummies every year (fig. 18). The sudden flourishing of this practice may have been spurred on by royal investment and temple building, particularly in the fourth century BC. Some of the associated temples are decorated with fine reliefs of pharaohs before the gods. Such animal cemeteries are found throughout Egypt, and burials of many species have been found, including cats, dogs, crocodiles, snakes, lizards, fish, falcons, ibises and baboons. As time passed, the variety of animals buried seems to have increased. These animals were not seen as unique gods, but rather were bred specifically for sale to pilgrims and pious individuals, as examples of a species associated with a certain god: cats for Bastet, falcons for Horus, ibises or baboons for Thoth, and so on. Through purchasing a sacred animal mummy, a person would expect the priests to bury the animal with others of its kind, and thus gain access to the god associated with that animal. In many ways, it might have been similar to the practice of purchasing a bronze figurine. These burials happened at regular intervals, often on the days of

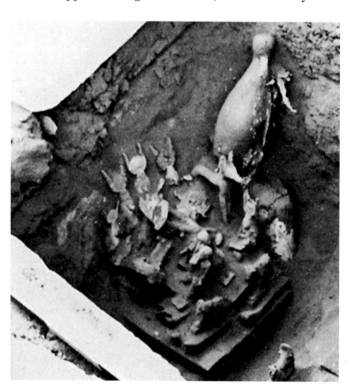

19 Cache of bronzes found at North Saqqara, c. 4th century BC.

specific religious festivals, after which the catacombs were sealed up.

Some gods could be approached with specific questions by pilgrims, and the movement or reaction of the god's statue was interpreted by the priests as a sign from the god in favour of a solution to the question. The most famous oracles were those of unique divine animals, such as the Buchis bull. Pilgrims would sometimes sleep overnight at the temple, in specially prepared spaces, in the hope that the god would come to them in a dream and respond to their plea. It has been suggested that the cult of these sacred animals was further connected to Osiris, the principal god of the afterlife, and also the king. Egyptian religion is notable for its ability to support several concurrent interpretations, even seemingly contradictory ones.

The sacred animal cemeteries were accompanied by temples with attendant priests, animal breeding areas and workshops to produce the coffins and mummification materials. A crocodile-egg hatchery may have been found in the Fayum, and administrative texts on papyri refer to areas where ibis eggs were to be incubated, and even the birds' 'feeding places'. Some of the texts reveal that corruption and negligence were not unknown in these sacred animal complexes: we know of one investigation into the theft of feed for sacred ibises, which led to the death through starvation of some of the birds. Similar arrangements and problems must have existed at cat cemeteries.

Examination of cat skeletons from sacred animal cemeteries showed evidence of strangulation, with most aged between one and four months or nine and twelve months, though this may not have been commonplace before the fourth century BC. In other cases, it seems that the cats were killed by a heavy blow to the head. Such culls would have reduced the number of cats who had reached sexual maturity, thus helping to control numbers. Were there special buildings for these mass killings? At Saqqara, the vast majority of buried cats were clearly intentionally bred domesticated cats, though occasional examples of wild cats have been identified. The cats were generally eviscerated after death, but the most important part of the process was the drying of the corpse using natron and perhaps sand. The dried body was often covered in a thick black substance made of a combination of materials such as resin, oil, pitch and bitumen; these slowed bacterial growth, which was crucial when the body had not been thoroughly dried. Experiments suggest that the drying process could have taken up to twenty days for a small animal such as a cat.

The body was then wrapped in linen bandages, themselves often soaked in resin. In some cases, the cat's limbs were all wrapped separately, producing a mummy very close in shape to that of the living animal, with clearly defined limbs, tail and head. More typically, cats were mummified with their rear legs tucked up behind the body, or with the tail brought up between their rear legs, allowing a neat package to be made. The linen wrappings were often finely arranged to create patterns, especially in the Roman Period (fig. 20), and the shape of a cat's head could be modelled in the linen. X-rays of the mummies have also

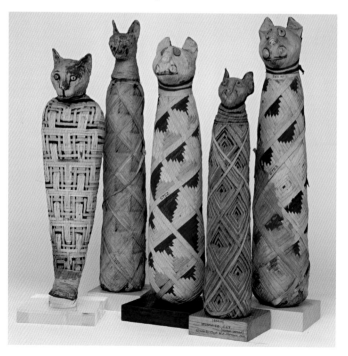

20 Cat mummies of the Roman era (1st century BC–2nd century AD), that on the left from Abydos.

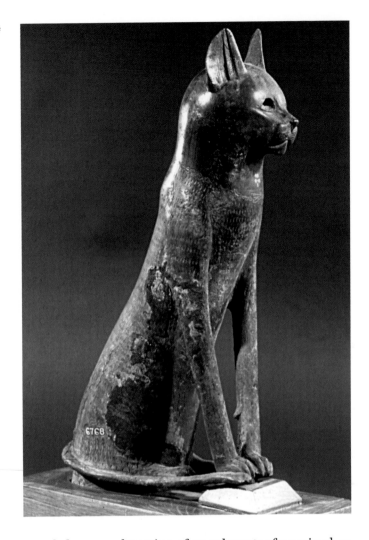

21 Bronze coffin in the form of a cat, still containing parts of a mummy. From Abusir, 4th–1st century BC.

revealed some malpractice: often only parts of an animal, or a mixture of several, were placed inside the linen bandages. Returning to the better-documented ibis cult, there is an interesting reference to the desired burial being 'one god in one vessel'. However, of over 270 cat mummies studied from the excavations at the Bubastieion in Saqqara, nearly a third proved to contain no parts of cats at all! The buyer would probably not have been aware of this, and it may not even have been considered necessary to have a complete animal.

The linen-wrapped package would then be placed in a coffin, or simply in a pottery jar. Many coffins took the form of a seated cat, whether in bronze or, more commonly, wood: the Egyptians cleverly took advantage of the natural form of the cat to produce a lifelike figure whose lower body doubled up as a container (fig. 21). The means of the person paying for the burial would presumably have dictated the quality and materials of both the mummification and any coffin, whether pottery, wood or bronze. Bronze coffins were often embellished with precious-metal inlays and rings.

If the Gayer-Anderson Cat was from an animal cemetery, whether set up in one of the temples or used to hold a mummy, where is it likely to have come from? The Greek historian Herodotus indicated that all sacred cats were to be brought to Bubastis in the Delta for burial, falcons to Buto and ibises to Hermopolis, on the basis of information collected during his visit to Egypt around 450 BC. Sadly, the cat cemetery at Bubastis was almost completely destroyed before it could be studied properly. Bubastis was the site of one of the main temples to the goddess Bastet, and by the first millennium BC, it was a sizeable city which hosted one of the best known religious festivals. Herodotus witnessed the festival and left us this description:

> When the people are on their way to Bubastis they go by river, men and women together, a great number of each in every boat. Some of the women make noise with rattles, others play flutes all the way, while the rest of the women, and the men, sing and clap their hands .... But when they have reached Bubastis, they make a festival with great sacrifices, and more wine is drunk at this feast than in the whole year beside. Men and women (but not children) are wont to assemble there to the number of seven hundred thousand.

Many of the bronze cats now in museums come from this cemetery, which was dug and looted throughout the late nineteenth century. Hundreds of thousands of cat mummies were exported to Europe as fertilizer and fuel. In 1885, the English banker and antiquary F.G. Hilton Price described the cat figurines from Bubastis in his collection, assembled by Clarke Bey, a friend who lived near the ancient site:

> many seated erect, with the tail curled round on the right side, wearing a collar, with a pendant in front, generally of the mystic eye, with a counterpoise behind; glass or crystal eyes; in many of the bronze heads the eye-sockets are hollow, indicating they have had crystal eyes, and in others the eyes have been sunk into recesses. Some of these cats are seated upon bronze pedestals. . . . Some of the cats have a scarabaeus upon their heads in bronze, others have had them set in glass or crystal . . . one of them has the scarab simply engraved upon the head. My largest cat is 11 inches [28 cm] high, hollow, and has probably served for a mummy case for a cat.

He noted that many of the figures came from vaulted brick 'wells' or 'pits' reached by passageways, probably brick-lined tombs or underground galleries. Along with a mass of cat bones, many bronze figurines were also found, including cat-headed women and images of Osiris and Nefertum. A number of bronze heads of cats were recovered, perhaps intended to be placed over linen-wrapped cat mummies (some of the heads still contained fragments of 'bones and bits of cloth'). Other cat mummies found at the site were simply placed in ceramic vessels, laid in rows; alternatively, parts of cat mummies were placed in small bronze boxes decorated with a small figure of a cat. Perhaps bronze and pottery were favoured in the damp conditions of the Delta, while wooden coffins were commonly found at southern sites such as Thebes, where the climactic conditions would help their preservation.

Hilton Price's description suggests that figures like the Gayer-Anderson Cat could have come from the cat cemetery at Bubastis, whether as a cat coffin or a statue to be placed in the tombs of associated chapels. But while there is archaeological evidence that some animal mummies were specially sent to certain sites, it is clear that from the fourth century BC onwards, if not before, cats were being buried at other sites too. In addition to Bubastis, large cat cemeteries have been found at Istabl Antar (near Beni Hassan) and Saqqara, all near major cult centres of feline gods. Cat burials in lesser numbers have been found at many other sites.

Much of the ancient necropolis of Saqqara was used for sacred animal burials, including cats, in the first millennium BC, attracting pilgrims from throughout the eastern Mediterranean. Large temple complexes at the foot of the escarpment, into which the tombs were cut, provided a focal point for pious visitors, and housing and work areas for the priests who managed the sacred animal breeding and burials, some of whom we know were involved in the cult of Bastet. Cats were buried in the tombs of important officials of the late 18th and early 19th Dynasties. These had been built and decorated many centuries earlier, but having been looted and fallen into disrepair were reused, saving the need to cut new underground galleries. Small amuletic bronze figures of cats were sometimes placed among the wrappings, and some cats were even placed in individual stone coffins. These tombs remained in use as cat cemeteries from around 400 BC down into the Roman Period.

Saqqara, and nearby Giza where many cat burials were found in the cemetery 1600 metres south of the Great Pyramid, are likely provenances for the Gayer-Anderson Cat, due to their proximity to Cairo and the dry conditions that would favour the preservation of metal objects. In the British Museum's *Report of Donations* of 4 October 1947, the Cat is described as being 'from the ruins of Memphis', but it is not clear what this information is based on. Whether true or not, it seems more likely that the Cat came from a temple, possibly one associated with a cat cemetery.

It is interesting that the apparent upsurge in the popularity of animal cults seems to have coincided with a period of several centuries when Egypt was ruled by foreigners: do these cults reflect a wish to express 'Egyptianness' in the face of outside control and influences? The burial of animals persisted through the Ptolemaic and Roman Periods, finally being outlawed in 379 AD with the Edict of Theodosius, which stipulated the closure of all pagan temples.

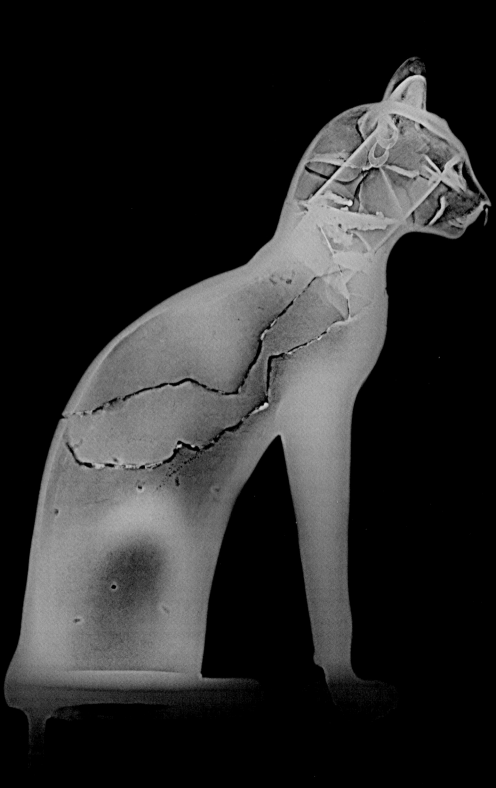

Chapter Four
Unique masterpiece: the manufacture of the cat

Metals in ancient Egypt

From Old Kingdom times onwards, expeditions were sent into the desert regions of Egypt, and the neighbouring territories of Sinai and Nubia, to obtain metals such as gold and copper. Copper makes up the bulk of Egyptian bronze objects, and would have been extracted from ores mined in the forbidding desert terrain east of the Nile Valley and in modern-day Sinai. Smelting of copper ores may already have been taking place by the fourth millennium BC. Records of quarrying and mining expeditions indicate that up to 17,000 men could be sent away for a month to work in gruelling conditions far from the towns and villages they lived in. However, most expeditions involved only dozens or hundreds of men. Metal remained a precious commodity throughout ancient Egyptian history, being used principally for weapons, jewellery and sacred objects (statues, cult equipment including censers, tongs and vessels, parts of coffins).

Most surviving Egyptian metal objects now in museum collections, principally bronze figurines of deities, date to the first millennium BC, but large statues of kings made from hammered sheet copper are known from as early as the 6th Dynasty (Pepi I, *c.* 2270 BC). A small number of very fine metal statues of the second millennium BC have also survived. The inherent value of metal means that objects tended to be melted down for reuse, and thus survived less well than stone objects. The papyri recording investigations into the tomb robberies prevalent at Thebes in the later New Kingdom reveal that the thieves stole objects of gold, silver and bronze, presumably parts of coffins, amulets and other burial goods, and divided them up among themselves. A subsequent census records the amount of various stolen metals, sometimes simply by weight, found in nearby houses. At Amarna, evidence for the reworking of bronze scraps in and around a housing area has recently been found.

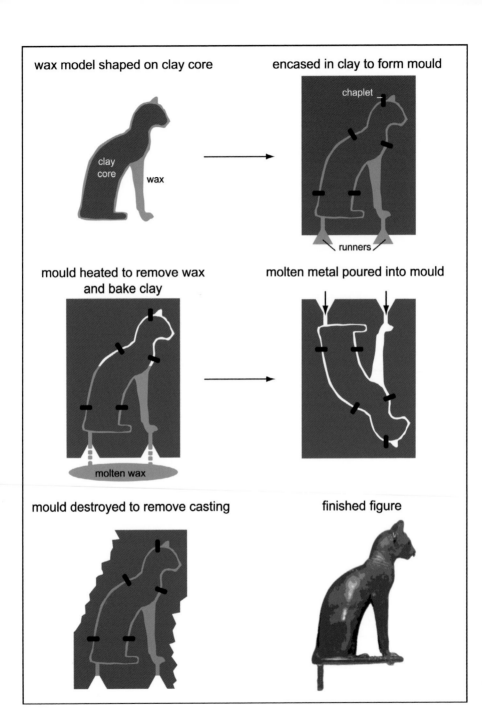

wax model shaped on clay core

clay core
wax

encased in clay to form mould

chaplet

runners

mould heated to remove wax and bake clay

molten wax

molten metal poured into mould

mould destroyed to remove casting

finished figure

The addition of lead to copper alloys, sometimes as much as 25 per cent or more, seems to be prevalent after the late New Kingdom, especially in the Late Period. Adding lead to the copper alloy would reduce the melting point of the metal, increase its fluidity when molten, and thus facilitate casting. This change may account for the large number of bronze figures produced in the first millennium BC: fine statues of kings and priestesses, sometimes up to 70 cm in height, and countless smaller figurines of deities.

Modern scientific methods allow us to measure the composition of the metal alloy used for the Gayer-Anderson Cat. X-ray fluorescence (XRF) analysis is a non-destructive process which can identify the presence and proportion of individual chemical elements in an object. Analysing the Cat is difficult, however, as the surface readings vary, perhaps because of the amount of modern treatments (including painting) carried out on the figure. This is a common problem with Egyptian bronzes in museum collections. To remove layers of corrosion, and in an attempt to stabilize ancient metal objects, some figurines were cleaned with hydrochloric acid, underwent electrolysis or were immersed in paraffin wax. A small sample of body metal provided a reliable indication of the composition of the metal alloy used for the Gayer-Anderson Cat: 84.7 per cent copper, 13 per cent tin, 2.1 per cent arsenic and 0.2 per cent lead. Individually these amounts are not unusual, but the combination of relatively high tin and arsenic levels, with very little lead, has not been closely matched in other Egyptian bronze figures. The addition of tin increases the hardness of metal, but, more importantly, also reduces its melting point, allowing smoother, high-quality casts. Arsenic, as a de-oxidant, lowers the porosity of the cast metal, but it is debatable whether it was an intentional addition or simply fortuitous. Perhaps the craftsman was looking to impart a paler hue to the bronze, a feature of arsenic-rich and tin-rich copper alloys? Within any given period, there is significant variation in the composition of metal alloys. While some craftsmen may have tried to choose the source of their metals, scrap metal would also have been widely available.

Copper Arsenic Tin Iron

counts

energy in keV

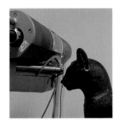

The Cat's rings were also analysed, revealing that the earrings were principally of gold with some silver and copper, while the nose-ring contained a lower proportion of gold. The discrepancy is not surprising, particularly as the earrings are undoubtedly not those originally made for the Cat.

Lost-wax casting

Study of ancient Egyptian tomb scenes and modern analyses of metal statuary have told us much about the process of producing such objects. The technique used to produce these statues was lost-wax casting (fig. 23), a method first recorded in the Old Kingdom. A model of the intended sculpture was first made in wax, or perhaps wax mixed with resin or oil, including details such as, for example, the scarab upon the Cat's head. If the piece was to be solid metal, a pure wax model would suffice, but larger pieces such as the Cat were more commonly hollow-cast, leaving a cavity inside the statue (see fig. 26). In this case the wax statue is formed around a core of clay. The wax figure is then covered with an investiture or casing, itself a mix of clay, straw and dung. The whole casing is then fired (causing the wax to run out) and turned upside down. Molten metal is poured into the resulting gap or gaps between core and investiture; the pouring points become the tangs of the final figure. Once the metal has cooled and set, the investiture can be broken away, and the fired clay core scooped out, leaving the near-finished statue. The artist still needed to remove any irregularities, particularly those left by the supports (chaplets) used to hold the core in place during casting, probably made of iron. These square-sectioned chaplets appear on the radiograph as small dark squares, and are clustered near the bottom, heavy, end of the statue. Finally, the surface would be polished. As the wax model did not survive this process of casting, each object is unique. Larger statues might be assembled from several elements, cast separately.

Metal casting, in this case copper alloy, was not straightforward, even after centuries of accrued experience. Faults could result from impurities in the metal, mistakes and breakages during the manufacture of the wax model, the casting process, and of course uneven temperatures reached throughout the whole process. The Gayer-Anderson Cat is clearly a masterpiece in stylistic terms, and the radiograph shows that the quality of the casting is very high: the metal areas appear to have very even density, with little porosity caused by gas bubbles becoming trapped in the metal while still molten.

The X-ray of the Cat reveals that the legs, ears and tail are solid metal, indicating that these elements were originally modelled in solid wax. In many cases, bronze cats' legs are hollow-cast, formed independently and either attached with a thick piece of wax (replaced with metal during casting) or actually cast on separately. Clearly, the maker of the Gayer-Anderson Cat did not have to be parsimonious with his metal. The tail of the cat is striped, using applied pieces of metal to create a banded effect. Analysis of the alternate bands, again using XRF, may have revealed an intriguing pattern. Interestingly, the three applied bands contain less tin and arsenic than the rest of the tail and the lower part of the Cat's body: did this create a perceptible difference in colour, with alternating bands of golden-bronze colour and a reddish coppery hue, enhancing the striped effect of the tail? Future analyses may shed further light on this part of the Cat.

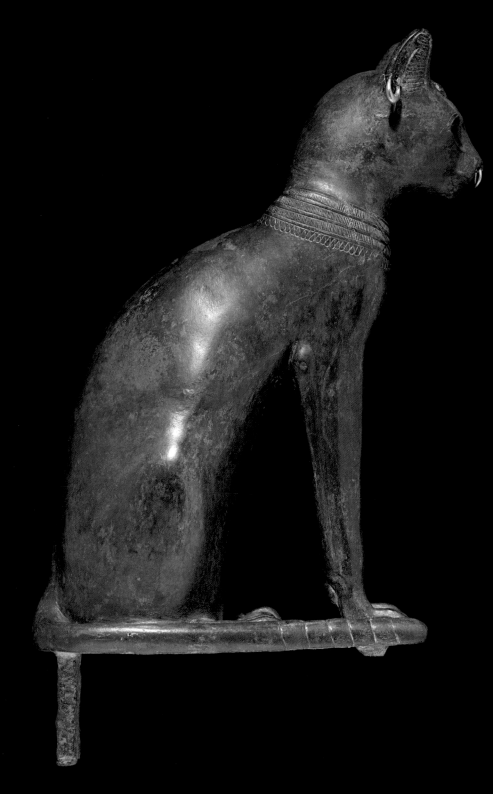

One of the final stages in the production of such a cat was inlaying additional elements. Eyes and plaques destined for inlay would often be provided with a stub at the back, which would slot into a hole on the metal figure to ensure that it remained in place. However, the radiographs of the Gayer-Anderson Cat reveal that it has no such holes, so the inlays must simply have been cut to the correct size and held in place with adhesives such as gesso, animal glue or egg whites. The silver *udjat*-eye plaque would have been inserted into the recessed panel in the cat's chest, a detail in the casting. The incised decoration, here including the elaborate collar, winged scarab and whiskers, would have been chased into the finished statue: viewing the pendants of the collar under a microscope clearly shows some of the tool marks. This method partly explains the unevenness of the incised decoration, which would have been much smoother if modelled into the wax prototype.

Metal craftsmen and their workshops

Due to the lack of well-provenanced and well-dated examples of bronze cats, it has proved frustratingly difficult to understand whether there are stylistic traits which are particular to one workshop, or even master craftsman, and whether the form of cats changed over time. The unique nature of direct lost-wax casting means that no two cats would ever be identical, but broad classifications could

26 *Right* The Gayer-Anderson Cat: underside showing cavity.

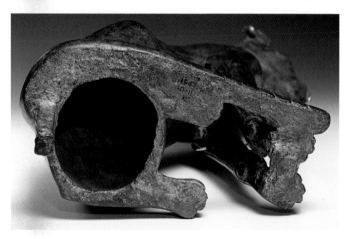

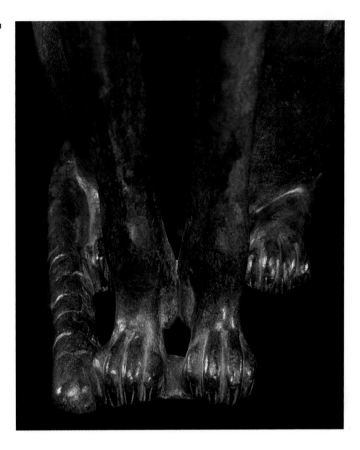

27 The Gayer-Anderson Cat: detail of the paws and tail.

perhaps be made. There are two broad groupings of the medium- to life-size cats: those that are rendered naturalistically, and those created with rather geometric segments, particularly of the chest and lower body areas.

It is unlikely that craftsmen of this quality would only have worked on cats; rather they would have been involved in producing everything from cats to figures of Osiris or ibises, whatever was needed in the temples and cemeteries near which they were based. We know that artisans who worked on statues, relief-carving and coffins could move around Egypt and this may also have been the case with the best metalworkers. A division between the production of such figurines and weaponry is more likely, particularly as weapons typically required a harder metal composition than sacred statues, so these may have been made in different industrial production areas. Of course, such work may have been carried out by a team of people: perhaps a master artist forming the wax prototype, others processing the metal (including heating it to about 1000°C in the case of a figure like the Cat and keeping the furnaces hot), forming the investiture and finally polishing and inlaying the figure.

Where were the workshops? It seems most likely that they were located near the temples at which such statues were dedicated. A few examples of metal workshops have been excavated, including a 30,000m² complex at the Ramesside city of Per-Ramses in the Eastern Delta. Crucibles, tuyères, moulds and large casting pits, waste products, slag and tools were recovered, all indicating large-scale copper-alloy production. Tomb scenes show men busy in metal workshops. These include depictions of ingots being delivered, melting the metal and pouring it into moulds. Craftsmen, whether metalsmiths, sculptors or otherwise, could also be attached to elite households or the royal court. Archaeological investigations can remind us of the dirt and waste produced by metal workshops, something not lost on the Egyptians. In one text satirizing various professions, written around 1950 BC, the metalsmith is described 'at the opening of his furnace, with fingers like claws of a crocodile, he stinks more than fish roe'.

The length of time it would take to produce a fine statue such as the Gayer-Anderson Cat is difficult to gauge. It seems inevitable that the craftsmen (or team) involved produced many more objects in their time, but we may never be able to identify these.

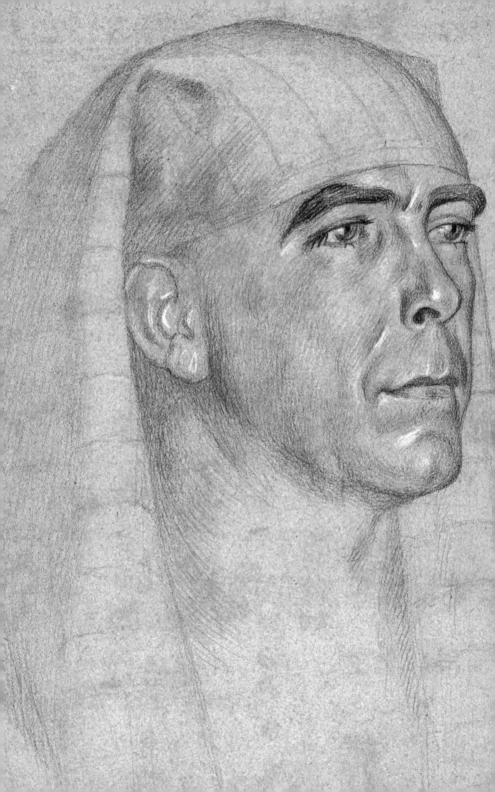

Chapter Five
An army Major, a medieval house, repairs and display: the modern history of the cat

28 *Portrait of John Gayer-Anderson as a sphinx*, by Sperling. 1928. Graphite and crayon on paper, 74 x 73 cm.

Robert Grenville 'John' Gayer-Anderson was born in Listowel, Ireland, on 29 July 1881. After medical training at Guy's Hospital in London, he joined the (British) Royal Army Medical Corps in 1904, which led to postings in Gallipoli (Turkey) and Egypt during the First World War. Retiring from the Army in 1920, as a major he stayed on in Cairo until ill health prompted a return to England in 1942. Although he did take on some posts in Egypt after his retirement, notably Senior Inspector at the Ministry of the Interior and Oriental Secretary at the Residency, much of his time was dedicated to collecting antiquities. His twin brother, Thomas, a colonel in the British Army, was an accomplished painter, and he completed several portraits of his brother.

Wishing to live in an old Egyptian house rather than in the new European-style buildings nearer the Nile, in 1935 Gayer-Anderson moved into a sixteenth-century abode next to the ninth-century mosque of Ibn Tulun. First seen by him twenty-nine years earlier when visiting the adjacent monument, the house was originally two separate properties, built in 1540 and 1632, later connected by a bridge. Known locally as the Beit el-Kritliya ('house of the Cretan woman'), it had been renovated by the Egyptian government over the preceding years. Gayer-Anderson was allowed to move in on the condition that the house and his collection of antiquities would be handed over to the Egyptian government upon his death or departure. The house is a fabulous example of domestic architecture from early Ottoman Egypt, with its finely carved doorways, spacious courtyards, loggias and receptions rooms, adorned with marble fountains and roofed with coffered wooden ceilings. Typical finely carved *mashrabiyya* window-screens offered the inhabitants a glimpse of the streets outside without letting passers-by see in. The house complex also includes a *sabil*, a public drinking fountain

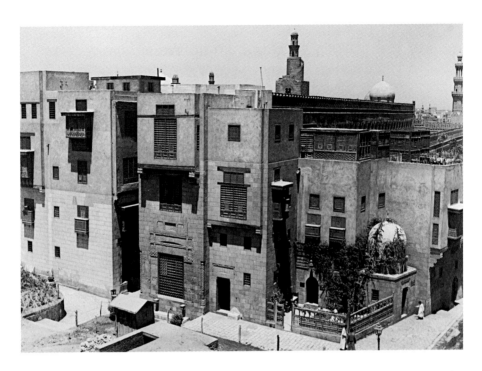

29 The Gayer-Anderson house in Cairo, beside the mosque of Ibn Tulun.

which would have been filled with water from the Nile each day, and the tomb of Sidi Haroun, a descendant of the prophet Muhammad. In such evocative surroundings, it is perhaps unsurprising that a series of legends and myths set in the house developed over time, some of them based on episodes in the Koran. Gayer-Anderson recorded these myths, which were recounted to him by the previous owner of the house, Sheikh Suleiman el-Kretli, the guardian of the tomb during the 1930s. For example, the mound on which the house and mosque were built is described as the place where Noah's Ark came to rest after the Flood subsided, its final waters disappearing down the well of the house. One of the myths even relates how the area once hosted a pharaonic palace, though the ancient capital of Memphis was actually far south-west of this site. Legends more explicitly related to the house include a tale about a protective snake and its young that inhabit the house, and the belief that young men or women looking into the well would see the face of their lover.

Gayer-Anderson made several changes to the house, including the roof-terrace with turned wood screens, used as a setting in the James Bond film *The Spy Who Loved Me* (1977). He purchased architectural and decorative elements from other old houses being demolished during the ongoing modernization of Cairo, and even imported a whole room from a seventeenth-century Syrian house. He used the courtyards, halls, rooms and staircases to display some of the art and antiquities he had collected. Furniture, paintings, carpets, metalwork, ceramics, manuscripts, glass and various antiquities from the cultures of the Near East and the Indian subcontinent thus embellished the house. The Museum Room, on the third floor of the earlier house, is still home to some of the pharaonic antiquities in his collection, such as casts of New Kingdom tomb reliefs,

30 The Celebration Hall in the Gayer-Anderson house.

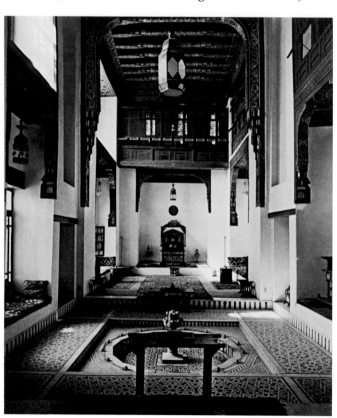

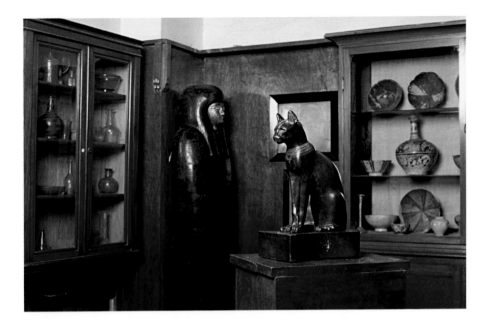

31 Cast of the Gayer-Anderson Cat in the Museum Room.

a 19th Dynasty coffin and a Third Intermediate Period mummy board, along with Persian tiles, pottery and magical bowls. The Cat, though now a replica, still takes pride of place at the centre of this room (fig. 31).

The Cat's twentieth century

Gayer-Anderson must have purchased antiquities from dealers and auction houses, as did so many of his contemporaries. It is likely that he encountered dealers during his travels throughout Egypt but, with his renown, dealers also would have come to him. A passage in his unpublished memoirs, *Fateful Attractions*,[1] describes Gayer-Anderson's first sight of the Cat, after breakfast on Monday 22 October 1934. An 'old friend':

carried a large bundle wrapped in cloth; but instead of the assured smile, usual on such occasions, he looked serious and wore an air of secrecy, almost of apprehension I felt. After accepting and lighting a cigarette, he confirmed me in the feeling by intimating that he would like no one but ourselves to be present when he showed

[1] All extracts from the memoirs are courtesy of The Gayer-Anderson Family Private Archives.

54

me what he had brought . . . squatting on a low stool close beside me, [he] very deliberately untied his bundle and began to extract from it a number of objects done up in newspaper and dirty clouts. These he unwrapped carefully one by one, handing each to me as he did so. [The objects] were so time destroyed and friable that I wondered why this man had brought these worthless relics and I felt a trifle annoyed at his having under-rated my standard to such an extent as to have done so.

Neither of us had spoken a word and it was dawning upon me that this man was probably building up a dramatic situation . . .. There was a long pause; he had stopped his unwrappings – 'is that all?' I was constrained to say and I knew that I was giving him his cue! – he did not answer but fumbling among the pile of wrappings on the floor, he produced another object – an object of some considerable size and weight. At last he disclosed the life-sized bronze statue of a cat . . . he held the bronze up to me with a dramatic gesture! Yes! This was the climax he had worked up to so skilfully and successfully.

I examined it carefully. It appeared to be whole and complete and it was covered with a heavy coating of reddish and greenish deposits which hid much detail and subtlety of modelling, but I have found with fine pharaonic bronzes that their beauty and merit are always patent no matter what their condition and this was no exception. To my practised eye it was obviously a work of the greatest refinement and beauty of form, a bronze of great rarity and value.

A price of fifty Egyptian pounds, 'a considerable sum for me to outlay on any single antique', was agreed with the dealer. After a month's delay, Gayer-Anderson commenced cleaning work on the Cat. His twin brother later described the figurine as:

so thickly covered with incrustations due to its two thousand five hundred years in the ground that its detail was completely hidden. John worked steadily on it for

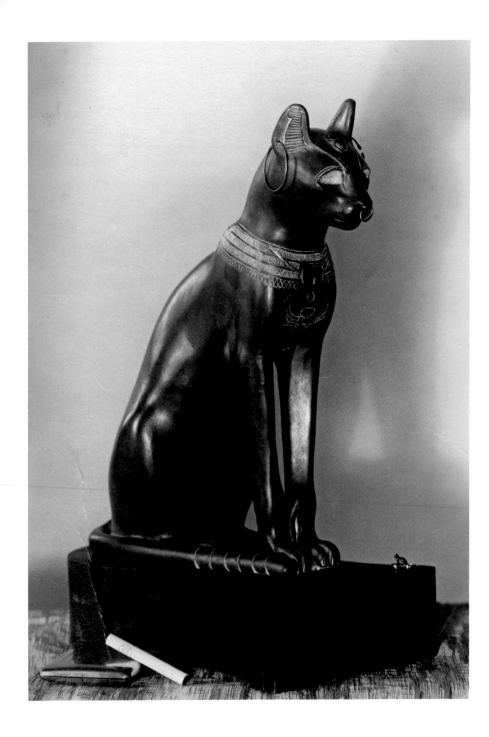

over a year, revealing by degrees the lovely simplicity of its modelling, its silver inlays and other ornament, some of it quite unique.[2]

Details of the process are given in John Gayer-Anderson's own memoir:

> I followed a technique in which I was already highly proficient from long practice and which if carefully and successfully carried out brings a good sound bronze such as this proved to be back to its original surface and condition. Using only a hammer, chisel and burner I carefully flaked off little by little the layers of outer grey-green and inner brick-red patines and gradually an exquisite figure of a cat emerged as if from under a veil that was being slowly stripped off her. The cleaning of Basht [Bastet] was indeed a labour of love – it took me over a year from the time of purchase to its completion.

Recent analyses undertaken at the British Museum show that the Cat may have been rather more damaged when Gayer-Anderson first set eyes upon it and how harsh some of the above treatment was. A large crack runs around its upper body, clearly visible on the X-ray image: a sizeable section of the Cat's back must have become detached from the rest of the body at some point, although the head may still have been joined by a few centimetres at the front. We do not know whether this is due to damage sustained in antiquity, or perhaps during its excavation. An elaborate supporting structure was placed inside the head, featuring what is probably a machine-made hollow metal cylinder with a hook at one end, and significant amounts of soft solder, which appear as white 'staining' on the X-ray. These efforts must have been an attempt to ensure that the Cat remained in one piece. Further packing material was added in the upper body cavity, making investigation of the repairs rather difficult. Two pins running into the back of the silver plaque on the Cat's chest suggest that this piece may also have been loose, and secured in place by modern repair. It is not impossible that the plaque is a replacement for a

[2] Preface by T.G. Gayer-Anderson to J.G. Gayer-Anderson, *Christeros and Other Poems* (London, 1948).

missing original. A contemporary of Gayer-Anderson's, Major Garland, also stationed in Cairo, co-authored a book with detailed advice for collectors of antiquities on how to clean bronzes and repair breaks, including soldering, inserting pins, filling hollows with plaster and using parts from other broken statues. The rings now sported by the Cat may have been added at this time. All these repairs and treatments were carried out with some skill as the extent of damage remained unknown until over seventy years later. A replica of the Cat had been made, presumably in metal, by Gayer-Anderson by 1939. Many years later the British Museum produced resin and bronze replicas of the Cat for sale in its shop.

The present-day appearance of the Cat thus owes much to what happened to it in the early part of the twentieth century. Bronze figurines were favoured by collectors because they were highly portable, and the deities depicted reflected the strange and exotic world of ancient Egypt: lion-headed women, jackals, snakes on boxes, male gods with tall feathers as headdresses. But copper alloy is very vulnerable to corrosion, particularly when it comes into contact with moisture. Excavated examples of bronzes nearly always have the resulting green surface. Gayer-Anderson's description suggests that the surface of the Cat was heavily corroded with 'bronze disease'. This corrosion can be exacerbated by excessive humidity, likely in the damp ground of the Delta at sites such as Bubastis. Analysis of the Cat revealed a layer of red cuprite (Cu_2O) lying beneath the green surface, presumably that mentioned by Gayer-Anderson in his memoirs. However, this green is not a copper compound commonly found as a product of corrosion, but rather a layer of polished green paint, applied in modern times to give the Cat its distinctive colour. Such a paint layer would also disguise the extensive repairs made to the figure. Collectors of ancient Egyptian bronzes frequently stripped, polished and painted their objects, perhaps in a bid to have them look more like those of the Renaissance. These treatments, which still took place in museums until the mid-twentieth century, often led to the removal of any results of corrosion, but also sometimes

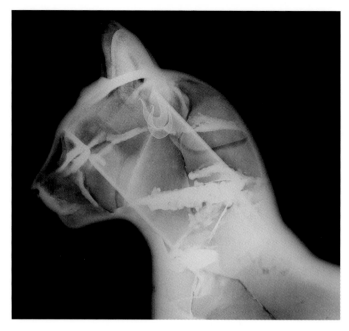

33 X-ray photograph of the Gayer-Anderson Cat: detail of the head area, showing later repairs and insertion of metal supports.

removed any traces of the surviving surface. As the original surface of the Cat is now lost, we will never know how it looked in ancient times.

According to his memoirs, Gayer-Anderson nearly sold the Cat, which had become:

> famous in Cairo and many people whom I had not even met came to see her . . . they fell in love with her at first sight and, as one can imagine, longed to possess her – several of the richer ones being anxious to buy. Amongst these was a foreigner who became so completely obsessed with the desire for possession and was so persistent that at last, though most unwillingly and against my better judgement, I yielded and agreed to let him have her for £2000 . . . to my intense relief, I heard by post from the prospective buyer that, owing to a serious financial reverse, he was forced to cancel the transaction. What glorious news that was! What a heaven sent deliverance! Basht (Bastet) and I celebrated it together and to mark the occasion I definitely decided to present the bronze to the British Museum.

Thus in April 1939 the director of the British Museum, Sir John Forsdyke, received a letter informing him that the Cat was to be passed to a museum upon Gayer-Anderson's death, although initially it would remain in the possession of the major's friend Mary Stout until she passed away. The accompanying photograph shows the appearance of the Cat at this time (fig. 32). If the British Museum would not accept the piece, it was to be offered to, in order, the Victoria and Albert Museum in London, the Metropolitan Museum of Art in New York, the Fitzwilliam Museum in Cambridge or the Ashmolean Museum in Oxford. Mary Stout (later Shaw), the daughter of a wealthy businessman, lived in Cairo during the 1930s. Gayer-Anderson was keen that she retained possession of the Cat while she was alive; a note in his memoirs describes her as 'an old friend . . . who feels most strongly that she has, in some former existence, been a priestess of or in some way connected with the goddess Basht [Bastet]'. Following the recommendation of Sidney Smith, Keeper of Antiquities, and the approval of the Museum's lawyers, the director replied to Gayer-Anderson that the Museum would be happy to accept the donation as long as it was kept informed about the whereabouts of the Cat while in Mary Stout's possession.

It turns out that the Cat was in a sealed wooden box in the vault of Lloyd's bank in Lavenham, Suffolk. With the outbreak of the Second World War, and heavy bombing in this part of England, Mary Stout became nervous about being in possession of the statue, fearing liability in case of damage. The Museum, however, refused to accept the donation at that time, as it was in the process of distributing its collections to safer places, including country houses in Nottinghamshire, a disused railway tunnel at Aldwych and shelters in Wales; eventually much was moved to a quarry in Wiltshire for further protection. 'Our policy is rather to divide the risk by dispersing the material' wrote Forsdyke; he also assured Gayer-Anderson that Stout would not be held liable for any war damages. The original *Deed of Conveyance* stated that Stout would owe Gayer-Anderson £600 in the event of any damage to the Cat.

Following Gayer-Anderson's death on 16 June 1945, his twin brother, Thomas, acted as executor to his estate.

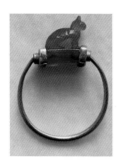

34 Gold finger-ring with carnelian figure of a cat, donated to the British Museum by John Gayer-Anderson.

Some objects were transferred to the Museum without fuss, including 199 coins, two ostraca and a silver figure of Eros, but the transfer of the bronze Cat and a small cornelian cat amulet mounted on a gold ring (fig. 34) was less straightforward. Correspondence between Thomas Gayer-Anderson and the British Museum continued through much of 1946 and the first half of 1947, with the Museum insisting that the original stipulations in the will could not be accepted in the post-war circumstances. These stipulations were as follows:

(A) That the Bronze Cat and the Cornelian Cat referred to in this Deed shall be displayed together as long as any Ancient Egyptian bronzes are displayed in the Museum (the cornelian Cat, on its ring, being placed on the front part of the bronze Cat's distinctive plain-wood mount) and that they shall be exhibited, if possible in a separate vitrine devoted to them only but failing that, in a prominent position in a vitrine amongst other Ancient Egyptian bronzes.

(B) That the Bronze Cat be known, described and catalogued as 'The Gayer-Anderson Cat' . . .

Museums rarely accept donations with attached conditions, as changing exhibitions over time do not allow guarantees about objects being on display for eternity, let alone in their own case. Despite protestations from Mary Stout, who suggested lending the Cat to the Museum if it would be displayed (a loan she was not legally entitled to offer), in November 1946 Thomas Gayer-Anderson agreed, in the light of his late brother's evident wish for the object to go to the Museum, to waive all the conditions except those relating to the name of the object and its plaque, which is still attached to the base today:

The Gayer-Anderson Cat
presented by
R.G. John Gayer-Anderson Pasha
and
Mary Stout

61

After a short stay in a sealed box at Gayer-Anderson's London solicitors, the Cat and the ring finally entered the British Museum on 20 August 1947. Shortly afterwards the statue was put on display in the 'Fifth Egyptian Room' and soon became one of the most iconic objects in the Museum. Photographs of it, sometimes accompanied by a living cat, appear in many books on ancient Egypt. Postcards were already planned in 1950, and Mary Stout wrote several letters to suggest the form and wording on the back of the cards. In 1960, with evident exasperation, the then Keeper of the Department of Egyptian Antiquities, Iestyn Edwards, wrote that 'this cat, which is not the best specimen of its kind in the collection, has been a recurrent source of trouble from the beginning'. Though the latter comment echoed the difficulties of the bequest, the former view is simply wrong: of twenty-six other bronze seated cats in the collection, none can match the quality of modelling and detailed inlay found on the Gayer-Anderson Cat. Arguably, no finer bronze cat has survived from ancient Egypt.

In 1981 it was transferred to the central space in the Egyptian Sculpture Gallery (now Room 4). Following the building of the Great Court, which opened in 2000, it was moved to the Upper Egyptian Galleries once again.

Many of Gayer-Anderson's antiquities were donated to other museums, particularly the Fitzwilliam Museum in Cambridge, which received over 7,000 objects in 1943, 1947 and 1949. These included bronze figurines, stone statues and reliefs, pottery, ostraca, cosmetic equipment, amulets and scarabs, furniture, tools and weapons, attesting to Gayer-Anderson's fascination with ancient Egypt. The Medelshavmuseet in Stockholm also benefited, and a large collection of paintings was donated to the Commonwealth of Australia in 1954. The remainder of the Gayer-Anderson collection is still kept in the house in Cairo, which was handed over to the Egyptian government in 1942 and is today open to visitors.

Further reading

J. Malek, *The Cat in Ancient Egypt* (British Museum Press, 2006 [rev. ed.]).

E. Hornung, *Conceptions of God in Ancient Egypt: The One and the Many* (Ithaca NY, 1982).

S. Ikram (ed.), *Divine Creatures. Animal Mummies in Ancient Egypt* (Cairo, 2005).

B. Scheel, *Egyptian Metalworking and Tools* (Princes Risborough, 1989).

J. Ogden, 'Metals' in I. Shaw and P.T. Nicholson (eds.), *Ancient Egyptian Materials and Technology* (Cambridge, 2000), pp.148–76.

D. Schorsch and J.H. Frantz, 'A Tale of Two Kitties' in *Appearance and Reality: Recent Studies in Conservation*. Metropolitan Museum of Art Bulletin, 55, no. 3 (1998).

R.G. Gayer-Anderson, *Legends of the House of the Cretan Woman* (Cairo, 2001).

N. Warner, *Guide to the Gayer-Anderson Museum Cairo* (Cairo, 2003).

Visiting the Gayer-Anderson House
The sixteenth-century house in which Gayer-Anderson lived in Cairo can still be visited. A replica of the Gayer-Anderson Cat is on display in the Museum Room. Midan Ibn Tulun (next to the Mosque of Ibn Tulun), Cairo, Egypt. Open 9 a.m.–4 p.m. daily, with a break for lunchtime prayers on Fridays. Entrance fee: LE 30.

Little Hall, Lavenham, Suffolk, UK
A fifteenth-century house, home to the Gayer-Andersons and subsequently bequeathed as a hostel for art students. Furniture, ceramics, pictures and sculptures from their collection are now housed here. Open Bank Holidays and Wednesday–Saturday afternoons, 6 April–27 October. Telephone: +44 1787 248179.

Photographic acknowledgements

All photographs © The Trustees of the British Museum, courtesy of the Department of Photography and Imaging, except for the following figs:

18 © Egypt Exploration Society; photograph by Paul Nicholson.

19 © Egypt Exploration Society

22–24 and 33: Images provided by the Department of Conservation, Documentation and Science, British Museum. Diagram in fig. 33 by Antony Simpson.

28 Courtesy of the Gayer-Anderson House Museum, Cairo, and the Supreme Council of Antiquities, Egypt; photograph by Francis Dzikowski.

29 Courtesy of the Gayer-Anderson House Museum, Cairo, and the Supreme Council of Antiquities, Egypt.

30 Courtesy of the Gayer-Anderson House Museum, Cairo, and the Supreme Council of Antiquities, Egypt.

31 Courtesy of the Gayer-Anderson House Museum, Cairo, and the Supreme Council of Antiquities, Egypt; photograph by Francis Dzikowski.

Details of British Museum objects:

Frontispiece, 1–8, 22–27, 32–33: EA 64391 (ht 42 cm; width 13 cm)

9 EA 37977 (ht 98 cm; width 98 cm)

10 EA 1106 (ht 154 cm; width 92 cm); drawing by Claire Thorne

11 EA 9901/8 (whole object 46.3 × 70 cm)

12 EA 10016 (whole object 15.5 × 59.5 cm)

13 EA 65 (ht 143 cm; width 42 cm; depth 70 cm)

14 EA 22752 (ht 72 cm; width 18 cm; length 28 cm)

15 EA 64525 (ht 12.6 cm; width 3.6 cm; depth 2.9 cm)

16 EA 12589 (ht 17.5 cm; width 5.3 cm; depth 8.8 cm)

17 EA 22927 (ht 8.2 cm; width 2.6 cm)

20 (l to r): EA 37348 (ht 46 cm); EA 26847 (ht 54 cm); EA 6752 (ht 51 cm); EA 55614 (ht 45.5 cm); EA 6753 (ht 53.3 cm)

34 EA 64392 (diam. 2 cm)